The Alliance of the
Indianapolis Museum of Art

The Alliance of the Indianapolis Museum of Art
A History

Jane Graham

Indianapolis Museum of Art

Jane Graham is senior editor at the Indianapolis Museum of Art.

Published by the Indianapolis Museum of Art
4000 Michigan Road
Indianapolis, Indiana 46208-3326
www.imamuseum.org

ISBN 978-0-936260-86-0

Library of Congress Cataloging-in-Publication Data

Graham, Jane K., 1944-
  The Alliance of the Indianapolis Museum of Art : a history / Jane Graham.
      p. cm.
  Includes index.
  ISBN 978-0-936260-86-0 (pbk.)
  1. Indianapolis Museum of Art. Alliance—History. I. Indianapolis
Museum of Art. II. Title.
  N577.G73 2008
  708.1772'52—dc22

                          2008043330

Editor's Note:
Four of the five logos that appear in this book were first used on the covers of Alliance yearbooks. The large A enclosing a circular design—patterned on the design of the IMA's Sutphin Fountain—has been used since 1970, with occasional variations.

Sources for this history include Alliance yearbooks, which, with a few exceptions, provide a report on each year's activities and accomplishments, financial data, and a directory of members and officers. Other sources include meeting minutes, scrapbooks, and correspondence. These records are available in the Museum's archives.

Design: JMH Corporation, Indianapolis
Photographs of works from the IMA collection: IMA Photography Services—
    Hadley Fruits and Mike Rippy
Image processing specialist: Laurie Gilbert
Coordinator of rights and reproductions: Ruth Roberts
Indexer: Barbara E. Cohen
Printed in Canada by Friesens Corporation
This book was printed using inks that contain soya oil or linseed.

Mixed Sources
Cert no. SW-COC-001271
© 1996 FSC
FSC

Contents

Foreword

Volunteers have been the backbone of America's museums since the birth of the modern museum in the 1870s. The Indianapolis Museum of Art, founded in 1883, is no exception. The Alliance of the IMA, established in 1958 by thirteen members of the Art Association of Indianapolis and our former director Wilbur Peat, is among the most accomplished volunteer organizations in the history of U.S. museums. Its membership has included the crème de la crème of Indianapolis society, but these hard-working women and men have always shown that no task, however unglamorous, was beneath them. Their efforts have been visible in everything from elegant balls and antique auctions to phonathons, receptions, and study group bus tours, to the distinguished art experts who have come to speak in Indianapolis at their behest.

The Alliance insured that the IMA's reputation was bolstered during challenging chapters over the last half century, including the move from downtown to the Museum's ultimate location on 38th Street. By launching our retail operations with a craft shop, rental gallery, a resale boutique called the Better Than New Shop, and our first restaurant, members of the Alliance not only enhanced the Museum's image as a welcoming one, but raised significant funds for this burgeoning organization's needs. From operating fund campaigns to art purchases, the Alliance protected the long-term interests of the Museum, raising millions of dollars to sustain our efforts to collect and present great artworks. From the beginning, they supported the purchase of avant-garde works by modern and contemporary artists as the Museum endeavored to build this important collection. By providing $2.1 million towards the acquisition of seventy-five masterpieces of Japanese Edo-period painting in 2000, they helped catapult our Asian collection to the foreground internationally.

Beyond their all-important role in supporting the IMA financially, members of the Alliance have volunteered throughout the Museum's buildings and grounds, serving at the information desk, guiding tours, providing office support, and welcoming guests at openings and other events. At a time when the Museum could ill afford a sufficient staff complement, the Alliance was there.

The Board and staff of the Indianapolis Museum of Art join me in warmly thanking each and every member of the Alliance since its founding fifty years ago, and in acknowledging that the vibrant IMA we all support today has benefited enormously from the stewardship and advocacy of two generations of caring and devoted supporters in the Alliance.

Maxwell L. Anderson

The Melvin & Bren Simon Director and CEO
Indianapolis Museum of Art

Acknowledgments

Many individuals contributed to this history. Linda Charbonneau, Gail McDermott-Bowler, Marian Meditch, Patricia Ritz, Roberta Walton, and Anna White—all past Alliance presidents—read the manuscript and offered not only valuable suggestions for improving the narrative, but encouragement. Alliance president Ginger Hoyt was an important advisor throughout; her patience and cheerfulness are appreciated. Linda, Fran Harman, Jody McLane, and Maeg Shackleton lent newspaper clippings, photographs, and other memorabilia that have been especially helpful in telling the Alliance story. Fran's written account of the beginning of the Better Than New Shop, now part of the Alliance archives, was an essential resource. Alliance presidents, other officers, and committee chairs kept meticulous records over the years, including meeting minutes, correspondence, scrapbooks, yearbooks, directories and account books; this history would not have been possible without them.

Appreciation is also due to IMA Photography Services, whose skill and dedication is evident throughout the book; to the staffs of the IMA's Stout Reference Library and Dutton Educational Resource Center, who were always ready to provide research assistance; to Noelle Pulliam and David Chalfie, who read the text and offered improvements; and to Michael Hayes, who created the elegant design for the book.

And many thanks to Maxwell Anderson, the Melvin & Bren Simon Director and CEO, and Sue Ellen Paxson, deputy director of collections and programs at the IMA, for supporting the publication of this book in conjunction with the celebration of the IMA's 125th anniversary.

J.G.

The new officers of the Herron Museum Alliance, elected April 18, 1963: (from left) Athena Wright, treasurer; Kay DeBoest, president; Fran Harman, recording secretary; Maxie Schnicke, corresponding secretary; and Gladys Dustman, vice president. Courtesy of the *Indianapolis Star*.

When the founding members of the Alliance began to envision the good they could do for their Museum and city, they could not have foreseen the remarkable accomplishments to come over the next five decades, or the group's extraordinary longevity. In just a few years the Alliance developed into one of the most successful volunteer organizations in the history of Indianapolis, bringing new members and support to the Museum, raising millions of dollars for art acquisition, and bolstering the Museum financially in numerous other ways through long-term projects and special events. The Museum was at a turning point in the late 1950s, and the Alliance stepped up to provide leadership.

The First Year

On Wednesday, September 17, 1958, according to the carefully typed minutes that serve as a record of the event, a meeting was held at the John Herron Art Institute under the direction of Mrs. Booth Tarkington (Josephine Cowgill) Jameson and Mr. Wilbur Peat "for the purpose of forming a civic group to further the effectiveness of the John Herron Art Museum as a cultural center of the city." Peat was the director of the Museum, and Jameson was a sustaining member of the Art Association of Indianapolis and served as its public relations secretary. The other participants were listed by their last names only: "Mesdames Wade, Herrington, Klausmeyer, Brant, Gerdan, Buschmann, DeVault, Faries, Wells, Welliver, Carmichael and Ansted."* Beverly Carmichael and Virginia Ansted were named temporary chairman and secretary.

  With an enthusiasm that would characterize them over the years—and with suggested bylaws written by Peat—they immediately began to focus on events and projects that they could organize to "stimulate interest in the Herron collections, exhibitions and programs." They also considered names for the group—some with a decidedly French flavor, such as "Herron Belle Arts," "Quatre Arts" and "D'Ami Arts"—and each person presented a list of candidates for membership, which was by invitation only in the early years. There were eventually forty-eight charter members.

*The following names were found in early Alliance yearbooks: Agnes Wade, Nell Herrington, Jane Klausmeyer, Tina Brant, Esther Gerdan, Betty Buschmann, Jeanne DeVault, Betty Wells, Janet Welliver, Beverly Carmichael and Virginia Ansted.

At the next meeting, on September 25, Carmichael, who had been associated with a similar group in Kansas City, "pointed out that the new John Herron group should be a working one—that would help the Art Museum." She also talked about fundraising projects, how "an author, a dance or similar activities would do much to aid the Museum in planning its programs, adding to its collections and exhibitions." Dues were set at $10 for a couple and $5 for individuals (both men and women were eligible), and membership in the Art Association was a prerequisite of membership in the group. Lucille (Mrs. Elijah B.) Martindale was elected as the first chairman (a title later changed to "president"), and the other officers were Virginia (Mrs. William B.) Ansted, vice-chairman; Betty (Mrs. C. Severin) Buschmann, secretary; and Esther (Mrs. Dimitrius) Gerdan, treasurer. Jameson, who is today honored as the founder of the Alliance, reiterated the purpose of the group: "to have more people know and enjoy the Museum, to use it and therefore support it." It was also at this meeting that Ansted proposed the organization's first official event, a cocktail party for the actor Vincent Price, who was to speak in Indianapolis on October 10 as part of the Sunnyside Guild's Town Hall

Alliance founder Josephine Jameson (right), with three former presidents of the group: (from left) Irving Springer, Betty Buschmann, and Lucille Martindale. Photograph from *Indianapolis Star Magazine*, November 10, 1963; courtesy of the *Indianapolis Star*.

Josephine Jameson and Vincent Price at a Coffee Chat in 1965. Price, an actor and artist, was the special guest at the first official event organized by the Alliance, a reception in October 1958. Photograph from the *Indianapolis News*, November 11, 1965; courtesy of the *Indianapolis Star*.

Series. (Two months later, at an executive committee meeting on November 19, Jameson suggested that the members plan some activities in addition to the parties, such as redecorating the cloak room at the Museum, gardening on the grounds, and assisting Herron art students at their spring exhibition.)

When they met again on October 24, the group had 103 members and a new name, the Herron Museum Alliance. And they were planning their next event, a reception for Richard H. Randall Jr., assistant curator of medieval art at the Cloisters for The Metropolitan Museum of Art, who spoke at the Museum on the topic of Romanesque Spanish frescoes. (Randall later served as the director of the Walters Art Gallery, Baltimore, from 1965 to 1981.)

By early 1959, the Alliance had a rapidly expanding membership and, more importantly, an energy that would propel it forward for the next fifty years. In the Alliance yearbook for 1962-1963, one paragraph lists some of the other accomplishments of that first year:

> Early in '59 Catherine Mattison [an artist, and the wife of the art school director, Donald Mattison] donated a flower painting, which was raffled. The profits were used to found the Alliance's Fine Arts Fund. Also that winter, the Alliance undertook to oversee the refreshments at Coffee Chats, had a booth at the Home Show designed to lure people Museum-wards, helped start the Glendale Art Fair, and helped to increase the Art Association's membership by demonstrating that the pursuit of culture can be gay.

It was at the March 5, 1959, meeting that the art sale at Glendale Shopping Center was first mentioned. It was to be a "sidewalk sale . . . of works of John Herron students, faculty, and alumni." The event, scheduled for May 20, included prizes for the artists, and the members saw it as an opportunity to promote the Art Association and the Alliance. Activities such as the art fair were apparently scrutinized for their fundraising potential, which was important to the members from the beginning. In October 1961, at an executive committee meeting, the Glendale Art Fair was one of the topics for discussion, particularly the fact that it brought no money into the organization. However, "it was felt that it was excellent public relations and an opportunity to be of service, and it was voted again to participate in the Fair."

In less than a year, the newly formed organization had projects and a vision, and according to records of the meeting on May 7, 1959, a balance of $625 (estimated) and 221 members.

The Art Rental Gallery

The Alliance membership roster and its treasury steadily increased over the next few years as the group organized more activities and fundraising events. One of those projects was the Art Rental Gallery, which opened in October 1960 in the Museum's cloak room—recently redecorated by Alliance members. It was the first of the Alliance's very successful and long-standing "businesses," generating a steady stream of income that would be used to benefit the Museum for more than forty years. Individuals and companies could rent or buy art from the gallery, and works that were offered for sale or rent—all by artists living in the state or with some connection to Indiana—were first approved by a selection committee. When the project was proposed, one of the group's officers had voiced her concern that the rental gallery "presented many problems." One concern was insuring the works, which would be given to the gallery on consignment by the participating artists. According to the minutes of that meeting, on May 5, 1960, the group agreed to continue with plans for the gallery, however, since the project "had been requested by the Museum's Executive Board."

At the meeting on September 15, 1960, the details of the gallery were announced: It would be open October through March, Tuesday through Sunday, from 1:00 to 5:00 p.m., and Friday evenings. Works could be rented for two months and renewed one time. The rental payments were applied to the purchase price if a customer decided to buy a work. The group's vice president, Esther Gerdan, reported that letters had been sent to "Indiana artists whose work has been exhibited in juried shows, and responses are already coming in." The group was optimistic about the prospects for the gallery, and Gerdan even expressed the view that it would be such a reliable source of income that no other fundraising activities might be needed. Forty-seven volunteers had been recruited to staff the gallery, and a selection committee was named. All were no doubt encouraged by the success of the opening week, when sixteen works were rented and two were sold.

In its earliest days, the contemporary works in the Rental Gallery were viewed as an important adjunct to the art offered in the Museum's galleries. In a defense of contemporary art, published in the Museum's *Bulletin* for spring 1962, Wilbur Peat wrote about the "lack of examples of the more advanced works by native or European artists, men and women who will become 'old masters' in the minds of future generations." He lauded the newly formed Contemporary Art Society for their efforts in filling this gap, and also cited the Rental Gallery. "Their policy of handling works by practicing Indiana artists has enabled scores of local families to enhance their homes with contemporary paintings, prints and sculptures, many of the pieces remaining permanently on their walls when a fondness for a rental item has led to a purchase."

A group of women who were early organizers and volunteers in the gallery, brought together by past Alliance president Linda Charbonneau in April 2006, reminisced about those early years. Charbonneau recorded and later transcribed the discussion. "The Rental Gallery was started by Nancy Woollen, Mrs. Carter [wife of Herron Museum curator David Carter] and Polly Taggert, who studied the rental galleries at the Toledo museum and the Chicago art museum, both run by full-time museum employees," said Ann Rohn, who worked in the gallery for 20 years, until 1979, and served as chairman or co-chairman during most of the 1960s. She noted that Taggert was a professional office designer and "we couldn't have had anyone better. . . . She and her husband worked hours and hours in the little cubby hole there in the stairwell, painting it and building slots for the pictures."

Polly Taggert, with art from the Alliance Rental Gallery. Photograph from the *Indianapolis News*, March 11, 1961; courtesy of the *Indianapolis Star*.

Six years after the gallery opened, a feature article in the *Indianapolis Star* (April 9, 1967), noted that eighty-five artists were represented in the gallery (about 250 pieces) and that about 100 items were out on rental all the time. All the artists were from Indiana or "had some experience in the state." Among the artists who were favorites of buyers and renters, the *Star* article said, were Rinaldo Paluzzi, Harry Davis, Rudy Pozzati, Martha Slaymaker, Claudine Paluzzi, Conroy Hudlow, Sarah Hurt, and Garo Antreasian. Many of them continued to exhibit their work in the gallery for years.

Others in the group organized by Charbonneau mentioned artists William Crutchfield, James McGarrell, Lois Davis, Amanda Block, Rosemary Browne Beck, James Wille Faust, Leah Traugott, Mary Beth Edelson, and Rob O'Dell. In addition to the money that the project raised, it was the support of Indiana artists that the gallery volunteers valued as one of their greatest contributions to the community.

William Richard Crutchfield, American (b. 1932), *Covered Wagons*, 1967, from the series *Americana*, lithograph with hand-coloring, 12 x 19 1/2 in. (sheet), Discretionary Fund 72.21.4. Crutchfield's work was offered in the Rental Gallery in its early years.

Businesses that rented and bought items during the gallery's early years included American Fletcher National Bank and the Indianapolis Athletic Club. Among the gallery's most well-known clients was Susan Bayh, who chose fourteen works from the gallery to hang in Indiana Senator Evan Bayh's office in Washington, D.C., in 1995.

Carl Weinhardt, the Museum's director; Donald Mattison, head of the art school; an interior decorator, and two art collectors served on the selection committee in the early years. In the organization's annual report for 1968–69, the eleventh year for the Alliance and the ninth for the gallery, Marian (Mrs. Boris E.) Meditch, the president, reported that the gallery had 100 volunteers and had realized a profit of more than $5,000 for the period.

After the Museum moved to West 38th Street, the Rental Gallery occupied spaces on both the parking and plaza levels before it eventually settled into its permanent home next to the Alliance Museum Shop. Maeg Shackleton, who volunteered in the Rental Gallery for more than thirty years—either as its chairman or volunteer chairman—said that the gallery "continued to provide a fundraising project for the Indianapolis Museum

of Art, to promote the work of Indiana artists and to provide a fine juried collection of art for the community." She noted that the concept of the gallery eventually expanded to include work by artists who lived and worked outside Indiana.

In April 1984, the Rental Gallery was host to the first midwestern workshop for rental gallery personnel, which drew participants from fifteen museums in the region and was the model for a national conference two years later at the Art Institute of Chicago. The most important event of the year for the gallery was the annual opening and reception for the artists in October, which was usually attended by 350 to 400 people. Another highlight for Shackleton was the "coveted Artist of the Month event." Selected artists were honored at Saturday morning receptions and had one wall of the gallery dedicated to their work.

Shackleton said that 125 volunteers worked in the gallery during her tenure, and she singled out one—Jean Mackey—for special recognition. Mackey served continuously as chairman or gallery advisor from 1970 until the closing in 2002. Throughout its long history, the Rental Gallery made annual donations to the Alliance Fine Arts Fund and supported other Alliance projects. Shackleton estimated that the gallery contributed more than $400,000 for the benefit of the Museum between 1970 and 2002.

As the Museum began to plan for a major expansion and renovation project in the early 2000s, decisions had to be made about the use of space throughout the existing buildings. On January 31, 2002, Rental Gallery volunteers learned that the gallery would be closed, and

Rental Gallery volunteers Jean Mackey (left) and Pat Lachelt study one of the 250 works available to Museum members at the new Indianapolis Museum of Art. Photograph by John H. Starkey, *Indianapolis Star*, October 11, 1970; courtesy of the *Indianapolis Star*.

Bonnie Swaim (left) and Maeg Shackleton hang new works in the Rental Gallery. Photograph by Frank Espich, *Indianapolis Star*, October 11, 1993; courtesy of the *Indianapolis Star*.

ALLIANCE

there were no plans to provide another location for the project. On June 21 of that year, the Rental Gallery closed its doors for the last time.

The High Life: Black-Tie Balls and Antique Auctions

As any Alliance member could confirm, there was always more than one way to raise money and to enhance the Museum's image. In 1962 the Alliance began to organize the first of what was to become a series of biennial balls to benefit the Museum. The Goya Ball, held at the Indianapolis Athletic Club on February 9, 1963, after the opening of the exhibition *El Greco to Goya*, raised $9,100. With the proceeds, and money raised through the Rental Gallery, the Alliance purchased its first work of art for the Museum. The second "Fine Arts Ball," held in 1965—also at the Athletic Club and organized by the Alliance in conjunction with the Museum's exhibition *The Romantic Era*—netted $27,000.

Encouraged by the success of the earlier balls, the group conceived the Fine Arts Jewel Ball, taking this fundraising effort to a new level. Mimi (Mrs. Edmund C.) Walsh was chair of the event, assisted by Mary (Mrs. Donald M.) Mattison and Sonja (Mrs. Harrison) Eiteljorg. Custom jewelry designed by the studio of William P. Nichols was on display, and some pieces were modeled by Alliance members. (Nichols underwrote expenses of the ball for the "privilege of displaying the jewelry," making him perhaps one of the Alliance's first major corporate sponsors.) Paul Masson Vineyards, California, donated the "Emerald Dry Riesling," rubino and crackling rosé, and the menu included filet mignon and a "flaming Alaska dessert." Cliff Hall and his society orchestra, well-known in Palm Beach and Newport, provided the music. Emerald green, which was in vogue that year, predominated at the event, and hand-stitched green velvet jewel cases were given as favors to all the women at the ball.

The Times
Women's Pages
Edited by Virginia Hill

From left:
Jo Ann (Jody) McLane,
Beverly Carmichael,
Isabel Ayres, and Mary
Johnson address
invitations for the Goya
Ball. Photograph from
the *Indianapolis Times*,
courtesy of Jo Ann
McLane. © Gary Yohler,
Tiffany Studios,
Indianapolis.

The guest list—with names like Ayres, Ball, Hulman, Lilly, Clowes, Fairbanks, Fortune, Glick, McKinney, Reilly and Tarzian—was a roll-call of business and community leaders. The Jewel Ball was apparently the social event of the season, and perhaps nothing indicated that so much as the fact that the Indianapolis Junior League changed the date of its Forty-fifth Anniversary Ball so it would not conflict with the Jewel Ball.

Photographs of the party, held on February 18, 1967, appeared in the May 1967 issue of *Town and Country* magazine. (In the mid-20th century, and as it had done for years, the magazine covered the social events and leisure activities of aristocratic Americans, such as debutante balls and society weddings.) A photograph of Walsh, modeling emerald and diamond jewelry and escorted by two young men dressed like

Committee members show off one of the 250 green velvet jewelry rolls given as favors at the Alliance Fine Arts Jewel Ball. From left are Mary Jewell Duck, Mary Mattison, and Jean Penrod. Photograph by William A. Oates, *Indianapolis Star*, January 18, 1967; courtesy of the *Indianapolis Star*.

Buckingham Palace guards in red uniforms and bearskin caps, was featured along with other photos in the *Indianapolis Star* in the Women's World News section. The event raised $20,000.

The ball served as the gala for the Museum's exhibition *Jewelry and Finery*, which actually was inspired by the Alliance event, a rare occurrence in the Museum's exhibition history. Organized by Stephen Ostrow, curator of collections at Herron, in about six weeks, the exhibition illustrated the history of self-adornment in the eighteenth through the twentieth century with jewelry, prints, and paintings from the Herron collection and other museums and galleries.

In his preface to the small catalogue that accompanied the exhibition, Ostrow wrote:

> An exhibition which derives its basic theme from a jeweled ball is bound to be somewhat frivolous. Yet the surface glitter of both this show and the social event which it complements is but a thin veneer over an essential seriousness of purpose: the ball to draw attention to and raise funds for the Herron Museum Alliance Fine Arts Fund, the exhibition to educate, to bring to the public a history of high style during the past two hundred and sixty-five years. (Preface, *Jewelry and Finery: Eighteenth through Twentieth Centuries*, Indianapolis, Indiana: Herron Museum of Art, 1967.)

Mary Mattison (left) and Mimi Walsh, co-chairmen of the Alliance Fine Arts Jewel Ball. With them are Donald M. Mattison, director of the Herron School of Art (second from left), and Edmund C. Walsh. Photograph by Jerry Clark, *Indianapolis Star*, February 19, 1967; courtesy of the *Indianapolis Star*.

Mimi Walsh, chair of the Alliance Fine Arts Jewel Ball, modeling jewelry from the studio of William P. Nichols. Escorts are Notre Dame students Tim Creany (left) and David E. Walsh. Photograph from the *Indianapolis News*, February 20, 1967; courtesy of the *Indianapolis Star*.

Other balls would follow, including the Bal de Lumière, in 1969, the Oriental Ball in 1972, the Masterpiece Masquerade in 1998 and the Masterpiece Ball in 2000. While the balls were not as successful as the Alliance retail businesses in raising money, these events brought glamour to the Museum, attracting new members with the means to provide that support. In just a few years and with the help of the Alliance, the Museum had shed its image of a musty institution whose members would just as soon keep it to themselves, and had acquired a new vitality and a new reputation.

Alliance members also organized art and antique auctions and other fundraisers to add to their revenue, and their first efforts in this arena were meant to have a broad appeal. An auction and flea market billed as "The Poor People of Paris," (the title came from a hit song from 1956) on the grounds of the Art Institute on September 28, 1963, drew an estimated 8,000 people and raised a total of $11,157 for the Fine Arts Fund. The Alliance's efforts to obtain publicity for the event were successful, apparent in the full page of photos and an article that appeared on the front page of the Women's Interests–Society section of the *Indianapolis Star* earlier that month. Donations for the auction came from Alliance members and "friends of the museum," according to the article, which listed, among other items for sale, "a pair of French lamps that belonged to Mrs. Conrad Ruckelshaus;

Mrs. Joseph Cain's Hepplewhite hunt table; and an opalescent French blue tea service with which Mrs. Edward B. Taggert served tea."

The success of the first auction and flea market inspired others, including one in 1965, also at the Herron Art Museum, and a flea market held at the Oldfields estate on May 4, 1968, that drew approximately 10,000 visitors and raised $11,734. Alliance members were probably encouraged by the success of the first Penrod Arts Fair, called "An Afternoon at Oldfields," held there the preceding fall.

The 1970s brought a series of more upscale events. Arthur's Place, an auction held in the auditorium of L.S. Ayres and

Thelma Battersby (left), Marjorie Schulz, and Betty Solomon examine items donated for the Alliance's September 1963 auction and flea market. Photograph by John Foster, *Indianapolis News*, June 27, 1963; courtesy of the *Indianapolis Star*.

Esther Gerdan (left), Betty Buschmann, and Jean Miner, all past Alliance presidents, make plans for the Alliance 1965 fall flea market. Photograph by William A. Oates, *Indianapolis Star*, September 12, 1965; courtesy of the *Indianapolis Star*.

Company April 16–18, 1970, netted $36,000. Among the 300 items offered at the auction, which was conducted by Trosby Galleries, of West Palm Beach, Florida, were a vacation in St. Croix, a jade necklace, a dinner at Oldfields, tennis lessons, and a seven-foot juniper donated by landscape architect Mark Holeman. Trosby (which made $22,000 at the event) offered 20 paintings and decorative arts objects at the auction, which had a "King Arthur in Camelot" theme. The three-day affair concluded with a $50 per couple black-tie dinner, underwritten by the general contractor Tousley-Bixler, in the Ayres Tea Room.

In April 1971, the Alliance brought Trosby Galleries back to Indianapolis for an auction of fine furniture, silver, paintings, and rugs valued at $1.5 million. "This earned $12,000 for the Alliance and provided an opportunity for the people of the Midwest to add to their collections and purchase beautiful items for their homes," Alliance president Jane Dutton wrote in her report for the year. Trosby was the second-largest auction house in the country at the time, and the 250 paintings they offered for sale included works by Chase, Church, Bellows, Hassam, Chagall, Renoir, Dufy, Rodin, Utrillo and De Vlaminck (which brought the high bid of the event, $41,000). A highlight was a painting by Corot that sold for $37,000 to a New York dealer. The furniture included a Queen Anne pediment-topped secretary, an eighteenth-century English sideboard, and a Louis XV bombe chest. The outdoor auction was held in a 100-by-160-foot tent in the parking lot in front of the Museum, and 2,000 people were invited to the preview party on April 23.

Patrons of the Arthur's Place "champagne auction" inspect some of the hundreds of items offered. From left are Mrs. Ezra H. Friedlander, Mr. Friedlander, Mrs. John C. Fechtman and Mr. Fechtman. Photograph by Charles A. Berry, *Indianapolis Star*, April 17, 1970; courtesy of the *Indianapolis Star*.

A second "Fine Arts Auction" was held in May 1972, and again Trosby Galleries was the co-sponsor. Among the items offered for sale were French, English and American furniture, porcelain, silver, oriental rugs, paintings, and "objets d'art." Trosby guaranteed $12,000 net profit for the Alliance, and an additional $10,045 came from the sale of items donated by Museum patrons.

Other forays into the world of antiques and auctions included the first Alliance Antique Show, held in June 1976 in the Egyptian Room at the Murat Temple in downtown Indianapolis, and a series of four annual

Ann Forrest, Dede Nie, and Patty Acheson study an English vase in preparation for the opening of the Lilly Pavilion in the summer of 1967. Photograph by William A. Oates, *Indianapolis Star*, June 18, 1967; courtesy of the *Indianapolis Star*.

consignment sales that began in 1978. Exhibitors came from around the country but especially from the East Coast for the antique show, and the merchandise included eighteenth- and nineteenth-century American and English furniture and accessories, brass, silver, paintings, prints, quilts, fine glass, jade, and ship models. Speakers from Colonial Williamsburg and the Henry Ford Museum were highlights. The first consignment sale, co-chaired by Martha Stiers and Martha Ann Bettis and held in the Museum's garage, featured antiques, cut glass, clocks, porcelain and other items offered by individuals who were willing to share twenty-five percent of the proceeds with the Alliance to benefit the Museum.

Later, the group turned from antiques and collectibles to wine, organizing their first "International Wine Auction" in 1991.

The Move to the New Museum

By early 1967, the Alliance had begun to anticipate the move to the Museum's new home on Michigan Road. Ruth Lilly and Josiah K. Lilly III had donated their parents' estate, Oldfields, to the Art Association in 1966, and planning for the new building had begun. The group's annual report for 1966–67 notes that "members lent support to the Art Association in petitioning the Metropolitan Planning Committee over the zoning of Oldfields." In addition, fifty-eight docents were "immediately trained to start the touring of Oldfields."

Meeting minutes from February 16, 1967, reflect the excitement and eagerness of the members to play a critical role in the new property. The membership committee was preparing to launch a new-member drive, considering the "wider scope of activities for Herron Art Museum members prompted by the anticipated use of Oldfields, including guided tours of the home plus plans for a tea room and gift shop." A month later, on March 13, it was reported that "Mrs. Lester [Sallie] Ponder and Mrs. William [Ruth] Kothe are organizing a course for docents who will serve as guides to visitors of Oldfields." Eventually, 143 docents, all from the ranks of the Alliance, were trained to lead tours of the new Lilly Pavilion of Decorative Arts. During their first year, they served an estimated 10,000 visitors and added $8,875 in admission fees to the Museum's accounts. When Alliance members met again after the summer hiatus, Thelma Leander talked about the plans for converting the Lilly family's "Playhouse" into a tearoom and reported that she had begun to ask for bids for remodeling the kitchen and redecorating the house.

In the midst of the excitement about Oldfields and their new projects, Alliance members did not neglect their roles at the Museum on 16th Street. In his annual report for 1966–67, Carl J. Weinhardt, the new

Mary Meek (left), Fredal Lomasney, Bonnie Reilly, and Dorit Paul were among the docents for the Lilly Pavilion of Decorative Arts in the late 1960s. Photograph from the *Indianapolis Star*, November 2, 1969; courtesy of the *Indianapolis Star*.

Alliance members display examples of the 800 Children's Creative Art Kits assembled by the organization to support the education efforts of the Herron Museum. From left are Louise McIntyre, Dorothy Maxwell, Susan Shields, and Mary Masters. Photograph by William A. Oates, *Indianapolis Star*, October 9, 1966; courtesy of the *Indianapolis Star*.

director of the Herron Museum, devoted an entire paragraph to the organization. After noting that "the Museum is here to serve the public at every possible level," he continued:

> Our great supporters, the Herron Museum Alliance, under the chairmanship of Mrs. Willis H. Tomlinson, have made heroic efforts in this direction. They have increased their own membership by 104, and they helped bring 482 new members into the Art Association. They have operated and expanded the Art Rental Gallery, and have assembled and sold hundreds of Children's Art Kits. They presented our major social event of the year, the beautiful Fine Arts Ball, and sponsored twelve Museum receptions and twelve Art Association Coffee Chats. They presented a scholarship to the school, and contributed most generously to the fund in memory of former director Wilbur Peat, and to a prize fund for the Indiana Artists' Exhibition. What would we do without them?

Marian Meditch, in her report on the Alliance's tenth year, 1967–68, called it "an eventful, important and promising one." She detailed the "new ventures entered into"—not only the Oldfields projects, but the new Craft Shop at the Herron Museum and the formation of a committee for the Operating Fund Drive. The Alliance had also recruited another 237 members, bringing the total Herron Art Museum membership to more than 3,000. And the group had a savings account of $105,000. "With this substantial amount of money, and as outlined in the Purpose of the Alliance," Meditch wrote, "we stand ready to cooperate in any way requested with the Art Association of Indianapolis in the exciting future of our Museum of Art and through this means in continued development of our wonderful city of Indianapolis and our State of Indiana."

Weinhardt thanked the Alliance again in his annual report for 1968–69, just months before the scheduled opening of the new Museum. He highlighted two major gifts, from the Alliance and the Contemporary Art Society, which combined to "enrich our collection of contemporary art in an unprecedented manner." The gift from the Alliance included works by Bernard Rosenthal, Lee Krasner, Gerald Laing, Claes Oldenburg, Barnett Newman, Larry Rivers, and Philip Guston. That same year, the group gave $1,000 to the operating fund and $3,000 for a promotional film on the construction of the new Museum. It was also in 1969—the year that the Art Association of Indianapolis became the Indianapolis Museum of Art—that the organization changed its name to the Alliance of the Indianapolis Museum of Art.

Claes Oldenburg, American (b. Sweden), b. 1929, *Tea Bag*, from "4 on Plexiglas," 1965, screen print and Plexiglas, 39 $\frac{1}{2}$ x 28 $\frac{1}{4}$ in., Gift from Herron Museum Alliance, 69.36.1

Lee Krasner, American,
1908-1984, *Towards One*,
1967, oil on canvas,
68 ½ x 65 in., Gift of the
Herron Museum Alliance,
69.36.7
© The Pollock-Krasner
Foundation/Artists Rights
Society (ARS), New York

In her report on the Alliance's thirteenth year, 1970–71, the first one at the Museum's new campus, the group's president, Jane Dutton, stressed how vital the Alliance's contributions were at this critical time. She wrote that "1970–1971 has been a year of many changes, enlarged responsibilities, and more meaningful opportunities to assist with the work at the Indianapolis Museum of Art. This period might be called the 'year of the volunteer'—a time when the Alliance was called upon to do many new tasks in an effort to solve staffing problems, to ease workloads of staff personnel, and, in fact, to take over necessary jobs where staff and money were unavailable." And they had the numbers to do the job, around 1,100 members at the close of the year. Dutton mentioned the 200 women who staffed the information desks for a total of 1,548 hours; the Alliance's role in hosting the two member receptions that preceded the opening of the Museum; and the 1,144 hours given by Rental Gallery volunteers. Alliance volunteers also handled clerical work for the development office and in other departments. Dutton also praised the Lilly Pavilion volunteers, who gave 5,184 hours. For years, the Lilly volunteers not only served as hostesses, docents, and general caretakers, but they also provided fresh flowers (which they grew in a nearby cutting garden) for the house and organized the yearly holiday decorations.

TAKE ADVANTAGE OF US ·· JOIN THE IMA

While they were proud of the financial contributions made to the Museum over fifty years, Alliance members always emphasized the time they gave to the IMA as one of the organization's greatest achievements. Their day-to-day volunteer work was rarely the subject of features in the local newspapers—as the high-profile fundraisers and the shops so often were—but Alliance members contributed thousands of hours every year in all areas of the IMA.

Anna White, in her president's report for 1977-78 cited the $78,000 contributed to the IMA that year by the Alliance and then addressed the members directly: "There are both the tangibles and the intangibles to remember—knowing that dollars are saved because you worked, knowing that art objects can be purchased because you gave of your time, and knowing that special opportunities for learning, for relaxing, and for enjoyment are possible because you cared."

In her annual report for 1981–82, Alliance president Dorothy Miller calculated the value of the 62,120 donated hours at $3.25 per hour, the minimum wage at the time, calling it "equivalent to a gift of $201,890 to

"Go Ahead! Take Advantage of Us" was the theme of the Alliance membership drive in 1976. Eleanor Beisswenger (far left) and Mary Young (far right), holding sign, were campaign co-chairmen. Others who have been identified are Anne Greenleaf (second from left, back row), Ernestine Lambertus (third from left, back row), Fran Harman (kneeling, far right), Anna White, (center of second row, with scarf), Thelma Battersby (kneeling, far left), Maeg Shackleton (kneeling, fourth from left, in jacket), Louise McIntyre (front row, far left), and Lenore Rochford (second from right, front). Photograph by William A. Oates, *Indianapolis Star*, March 30, 1976; courtesy of the *Indianapolis Star*.

the Museum." And she added: "Not so easily assessed is the value of increased public interest in the Museum and its collections stimulated by Alliance activities. The organized concern and devotion of 1,200 volunteers must be considered a major asset to the Indianapolis Museum of Art."

By the early 1970s, the requirement that new members be nominated by a member in good standing had been removed from the bylaws, and membership in the Museum had become the only prerequisite. Former president Roberta Walton, in an interview in February 2008, discussed this emphasis on commitment to the Alliance mission rather than social connections. "They really put a lot of their time and energy just into the Alliance," she said, and noted that the members were not necessarily members of other prestigious civic groups. "They respected who you were, how hard you worked."

The Craft Shop

One of the new projects highlighted by Meditch in her report on the group's tenth year, the Craft Shop proved to be one of the Alliance's most successful ventures. At a meeting on June 5, 1967, Thelma Battersby reported on the progress of the shop, which was to be located across from the Rental Gallery at the Herron Museum and stocked with items made by local craftsmen. (Battersby and Betty King co-chaired the committee that launched the shop, and Battersby was a volunteer in the operation for many years.) In October 1967, with the new enterprise now open, she was able to report sales of $600 in the first two weeks. The store's name was later changed to "The Enchanted Owl Craft Shop," perhaps in honor of Battersby, a potter and weaver who was an avid collector of owls in a variety of mediums.

A full-page article, with photos, in the Women's Interests-Society section of the *Indianapolis Star* on November 26, 1967, included an interview with Battersby and a list of items for sale in the retail operation: silk batiks, wooden trays, ceramics, hand-woven table mats, napkins,

scarves and stoles, enameled jewelry and ash trays, and stained-glass decorative objects. "This is an Alliance project," Battersby explained, "and all of our profits will be given to the Museum. We also initiated the shop as an outlet for the craftsmen in the area who have so few channels for their work." The Alliance bought the items at wholesale or took them on consignment.

Among the artists who sold their work through the shop during its early years were Mari Eagerton, Brenda Hayes, Jackie Lacy, Kay McCrary, Megan Rohn, Arthur Davis, and Aaron Rubenstein. Others were Bill Farrell, Karl Martz, and Dick Hay, all of whom taught in the fine arts departments at universities around the state. The works included both utilitarian and decorative objects, and covered the range of media, from clay, wood, glass and fiber to paper, silk, and plastic.

The Alliance Museum Shop after the merger of the Craft Shop with two other Museum shops in 1975. IMA archives.

Once the shop had moved into its space at the new Indianapolis Museum of Art in 1970, the volunteers initiated a series of demonstrations by craftsmen and, later, small exhibitions of works by featured artists. The monthly exhibitions, in Long Gallery, continued until the shop closed temporarily for construction of the new museum building in December 2004.

In 1975, the shop was merged with the Museum's separate gift shop and bookstore as the Alliance Museum Shop, in a 2,400-square-foot space on the parking level. Battersby was still crafts buyer in 1980 when she wrote an article for the January issue of *The Crafts Report*. She mentioned that shop sales had exceeded $250,000 for each of the previous two years and noted the "joy and satisfaction we have had in bringing so much fine craft work to the attention of a wider and wider audience." By then, the shop was offering the work of 300 craftspeople, half of them from Indiana. Crafts comprised about fifty percent of the space in the shop, while art books and commercial items occupied the rest. Battersby also noted in the *Star* article that the shop had one paid employee, Judith Grimes, and 200 volunteers, some of whom worked as many as twenty-five hours per week. Grimes served as the coordinator of the Alliance Museum Shop for more than thirty years and was still assisting at the store in 2008 as a volunteer.

Among the Alliance Museum Shop's most venerable volunteers were Anne Greenleaf, the longtime book buyer; Jane Lookabill, who succeeded Linda Charbonneau as business manager and served for more than twenty years; and Jeanne Scofield, who succeeded Battersby as craft buyer and served in the position for more than twenty years. Marian Meditch, the first commercial buyer for the Shop, was succeeded by Anna White. Roberta Walton, White's assistant beginning in the early 1980s, later became the commercial buyer, serving for more than twenty years in all. Others who served in key roles were Marion Helmen, shop manager; Nancy Bratt, receiving and marking; and Anne Throop, the Shop's last business manager. The Museum Shop flourished under Alliance management and was always a reliable source of income, as well as an essential amenity for Museum visitors.

The Alliance Garden Pavilion: Getting into the Restaurant Business

With hundreds of members with a wide range of talents and interests, the Alliance was able to support multiple projects. One particularly ambitious undertaking involved the transformation of the recreation house (the so-called Playhouse) on the Oldfields estate into a small restaurant. In her president's report for the year 1969–70, Jane Dutton noted that a committee had just completed two years of renovation and redecorating of the building and that it now had a "charming dining room that seats 100 people" and a new stainless steel kitchen.

At a meeting of the Alliance board on June 11, 1970, the Alliance Garden Pavilion Food Service and House committees were congratulated on the completed renovation, which had cost $75,000. "The renovation was well worth the money spent. Everyone found it difficult to realize that this large task had been accomplished." But, as the members would soon learn, there was more work to be done.

Just a year later, Dutton wrote again about the project in her report as president for 1970-71: "Although many difficulties were experienced, the beautiful building attracted large numbers of people whenever open, and provided food service for large groups here from out of town to tour the Museum." But the restaurant was forced to close on June 1, 1971, because of the "necessity to enlarge the kitchen area and install a dumb-waiter and restaurant dish-washing equipment."

From the beginning, problems had plagued the two committees that were managing the project. At the board meeting on June 11, 1970, Maude Fenstermaker reported that the tearoom, as it was called then, would use "volunteer waitresses, hostesses, and cashiers." Fenstermaker's committee had considered contracting with ARA Professional Food Service to run the restaurant, but they rejected that idea because of the cost. In October, Fenstermaker was able to report that the restaurant would open on November 3 and that Tres Bien Catering had been hired to provide the food service. The minutes include the comment that "the

Rita Hobbs (center), chair of the committee that refurbished the Alliance Garden Pavilion; Maude Fenstermaker (right), food service chairman; and Alliance president Jane Dutton in the newly opened restaurant. Photograph by William A. Oates, *Indianapolis Star*, June 13, 1970; courtesy of the *Indianapolis Star*.

kitchen is small and it will take time before the operation is smooth." The Alliance planned to hire waitresses, but would provide two hostesses and a cashier each day from their own ranks. A committee of the Alliance oversaw the operation and menu for the restaurant. Rita Hobbs reported on the building at the same meeting and listed equipment that was needed, including a stainless steel walk-in refrigerator ($900); bread warmer ($259); steam table ($400); and an adding machine ($150).

Less than two weeks later at another meeting of the board, on November 16, 1970, Hobbs reported on the lack of space for dishwashing. On a brighter note, Fenstermaker announced that there were "95 happy customers for opening day on November 3" and about 200 customers per day after that. Reservations were a major problem, however, and profits were minimal—just $691 as of January 1971. The group discussed applying for a liquor license to increase profitability. And it was clear that profits were needed. At the same meeting, Hobbs presented plans for an addition that would increase the kitchen size by fifty percent, at a cost of $23,000.

By the time the board met again, on April 12, 1971, a crisis seemed to be brewing. Fenstermaker reported that "while much time and money have gone into making the restaurant a success, there are still problems." The minutes also hint at tensions between the Alliance leadership and Museum management over the operation of the restaurant: "Cooperation

Kay DeBoest (left), Talitha Peat, and Josephine Jameson at the opening of the remodeled and refurbished Garden Room Restaurant in the Alliance Garden Pavilion. Photograph by William A. Oates, *Indianapolis Star*; courtesy of the *Indianapolis Star*.

is not always forthcoming. Relations with the accounting office are poor." There was even discussion of establishing an account for the restaurant separate from the Museum. To add to these difficulties, the reservations system was still not working, and the Museum had not yet signed the contract with the caterer.

The outlook was brighter by the fall. By the time the board met on November 11, 1971, the restaurant had a new catering company, Social Catering Inc. The Alliance would receive $600 in rent from the company and sixty percent of the profits. But just a few months later, the Alliance was working with ARA. Over the next couple of years, the restaurant would be self-sustaining, although not highly profitable.

The Garden Room Restaurant was closed in September 1974 "by mutual consent of the caterer and the Alliance at the direction of the IMA," according to Alliance records from the period. Those same minutes also note that "since the initial remodeling of the Garden Pavilion in 1969, the Alliance had supplied funds in excess of $141,000" to renovate and equip the building. The restaurant also raised $7,918.84 for the benefit of the Museum over the years that the Alliance managed it.

The restaurant reopened in May 1975 and was managed by a partnership that contracted directly with the Museum. While the project had never realized the fundraising potential that its supporters had envisioned, it was ultimately another success for the group. They had created an important visitor amenity at a time when the Museum could not afford such a venture and had persevered with the project in typical Alliance fashion and in spite of all the problems inherent in the restaurant business. The renovation was one of the group's largest contributions to the Museum during this period, and the restaurant would eventually become the popular Garden on the Green, a destination for diners in Indianapolis for many years.

The Operating Fund

While the Alliance's earliest efforts in raising money were focused on projects, such as the auctions and black-tie balls, the group became more directly involved in fundraising campaigns as the need for operating money for the Museum became more urgent.

In her report as president of the Alliance for 1969–70, Jane Dutton suggested this expanding role when she documented the success of the Museum's membership and operating fund drives during the year. "Over 600 women, working toward a goal of $30,000, accounted for 1,145 gifts totaling $44,933. Museum memberships increased by 470 this year, many the result of efforts of our committee, who sponsored a membership day at Oldfields in June." The Alliance also gave $16,500 from their own funds to the operating fund.

At a meeting of the Alliance board on September 15, 1969, Kay Strong, the operating fund chair, reminded those in attendance that they were needed for the fund drive, in addition to their other volunteer roles. The meeting minutes also note the "serious need for money" as the opening date of the new building on 38th Street loomed. At an Alliance board meeting on October 12, 1970, the members were told that "money is needed more than ever before to meet the museum's annual operating budget of $1 million." Less than a year later, in March 1971, the organization's bylaws were changed to include the requirement that all Alliance members participate in some phase of the Museum's annual operating fund drive. Over the next few years, the Alliance met the challenge, increasing the amounts they were able to raise during each subsequent drive.

The group's annual reports usually reflected the elation that the members felt at their success. In Dutton's report for 1970–71 she wrote that the operating fund campaign "was the most successful ever undertaken, in which 960 Alliance volunteers, working toward a goal of $35,000, handled 4,863 cards and actually accounted for $69,572" of the money received. In addition, the Alliance gave $10,200 to the fund. Fran Harman, in the Alliance annual report for 1971–72, called the operating fund drive for that year "a sensational success." She wrote that "$101,984.50,

Alliance president Jane Dutton (right) celebrates the success of the operating fund campaign with members Vivian Ammerman (left) and Harriet Albertson. Photograph from the *Indianapolis News*, February 19, 1971; courtesy of the *Indianapolis Star*.

representing 3,305 gifts, was raised because our members took our bylaws seriously and felt the responsibility to each doing her share to raise funds." And in the 1972–73 report, Harman gloated: "Those who said 'it couldn't be done' have had to swallow their words, for the Alliance Residence Phase of the Operating Fund has produced $132,016, representing 4,100 gifts." Later in the same report she mentioned that fourteen volunteers contributed more than forty-five hours to the Museum in a clerical capacity and ninety volunteers gave 1,402 hours to the Development office. The Alliance also increased its own donation to the fund, to $15,000.

At the end of the 1975-76 year, the group could again boast of success. Jeanne Scofield, in her report as president, documented the numbers: "Our excellent leadership in the Residential Phase of the Operating Fund enlisted 2,000 women to work. Their goal was set at $160,000, and they raised $175,000," representing a total of 6,116 gifts to the IMA. She added: "Reaching the Operating Fund goal is always an

Alliance president Linda Charbonneau (right) with Mrs. Donald Fasig (left) and Mrs. Patrick Towle at an operating fund campaign event. Photograph by William Palmer, *Indianapolis News*, August 14, 1974; courtesy of the *Indianapolis Star*.

enormous job, but so rewarding as the money raised helps keep our doors open and our Museum free to all visitors."

By the mid-1970s, the Alliance's Operating Fund Committee had twenty-eight members, one of the group's largest committees at the time. The Alliance recruited volunteers from women's groups in communities surrounding Indianapolis, adding hundreds of workers to the effort. But the amount raised diminished over time, and as the Museum's development staff burgeoned, fewer volunteers were needed to help with fundraising. In 1999, the requirement that all Alliance members participate in the operating fund drive was eliminated from the bylaws.

Ramekins and Rabbit Fur: The Better Than New Shop

The Better Than New Shop, the Alliance's longest-lived project, was the last of the four businesses started by the organization and a dependable source of revenue, particularly for its funds that were used to acquire art for the IMA. Fran Harman, who served as a chair or co-chair of the project for almost thirty years, documented the shop's history. It opened on March 15, 1973, with the name "Better Than New Cottage," on the day that the Alliance was having a regular meeting, followed by a luncheon in the Garden Room Restaurant. "After lunch the ladies all went shopping at the Cottage, located just east of the greenhouse in the Tudor double just off Michigan Road," Harman wrote. On that first day, the shop made $600, and it grossed $6,738 in the first two and a half months of operation. Among the items available on opening day were a silver meat platter, "Drop Rose" Haviland china, Chinese enamel ware, Limoges ramekins and a white rabbit-fur jacket.

Harman noted that Shirley Hale, whom she credited as the originator of the shop, and Lucy Miller were the first co-chairmen. Hale had

Alliance members (from left) Marian Meditch, Jeanne Scofield, and Mary Grady with Sam B. Huffman, promoting the "Under the Big Top" dance, a fundraising event, at the spring luncheon. Photograph by William A. Oates, *Indianapolis Star*, May 17, 1974; courtesy of the *Indianapolis Star*.

initially proposed the idea for the shop to her in May 1972: "a place where members and friends of the Museum could donate their items they no longer needed, such as antiques, collectibles and 'stuff' to be resold and recycled for the benefit of the Museum." Harman, Miller, and Hale talked over their strategy before presenting the idea to IMA director Carl Weinhardt, who was not only receptive, but also mentioned the Museum's urgent need for money to acquire art and for the establishment of an endowment to fund future acquisitions.

The Better Than New Cottage committee began offering their services for moving and estate sales in July of that first year. "Both Shirley and Lucy had done sales before and we were thrilled to open another avenue of funds for the Museum," Harman wrote, adding that these sales were another source of merchandise for the shop. Hale and Miller would do thirty moving and estate sales over the next two and a half years and finally asked to be relieved of their duties as co-chairmen. Katey Anderson and Elsa Wurster took on those roles in 1976, the same year Harman and Lenore Rochford became co-chairmen of the shop committee.

In 1976, the shop moved to Newfield, a house that J. K. Lilly Jr. had originally built for his son and his new wife in 1939, and its name was changed to Better Than New Shop. Ten years later, the shop was thriving and, even better, could boast of major donations made to the Museum each year. In her report for 1986–87, Alliance president Roberta Walton let the numbers speak for themselves. The Better Than New Shop had profits of $79,155.47, and of that amount, $37,272 was donated to the Fine Arts Purchase Fund and $41,884 to the Fine Arts Endowment Fund. She added that total shop sales for the past fourteen years—since its inception—had realized a profit of $766,264.73 and eighty-eight moving and estate sales had brought in $141,504.53, for a total of $907,769.53.

But the women of Better Than New did not use their impressive success as an excuse to slow down. In 1986 the clothing committee for the shop (sales of clothing made up about a third of the shop's income at one point) began modeling shop merchandise at the Garden on the Green Restaurant once a month. "Believe me," wrote Harman, "it makes a difference as to the income of the shop on those days, for they tell the customers about the shop, its location. Clothing is even sold during modeling."

In 1996, from September 28 to October 13, the Alliance, in cooperation with the American Society of Interior Designers, presented a designer showcase at Newfield, home of Better Than New. More than twenty-five rooms and other areas—from the wine cellar to the second-floor gallery—and the landscape surrounding the house were transformed by thirty-five interior and landscape designers. The project raised $9,582 from ticket sales and resulted in a much-needed facelift for the house and increased visibility for the shop.

In July 2003, the IMA honored Better Than New Shop volunteers on the occasion of the shop's thirtieth anniversary. Among them was Fran Harman, who had served unstintingly as a Better Than New volunteer from the shop's first day and energetically promoted it over the years. In May 2007, the Alliance honored Harman at the spring luncheon. The celebration included a song, "Hats Off to Fran," which ended with the words:

> So, take a bow, Fran
> You are quite a WOW, Fran.
> And it is so true—
> You're still better than new.

Fran Harman (right), longtime Better Than New Shop volunteer and past president, with Isabel Martin, Alliance corresponding secretary and former executive secretary to the IMA director, in April 2008. Photograph by Geordana Davis.

Several factors would finally cause the shop to close its doors forever in December 2007. The Museum needed the building for other uses, and the structure required major repairs. At the same time, the faithful Better Than New volunteers were retiring, and it was more difficult to attract new volunteers to manage the project. Over the years, Better Than New had done exactly what its volunteers had hoped to do. In her account of 2003, Harman wrote that the shop had given over $2 million for the purchase of art, all of it raised through shop sales and moving and estate sales—not bad for a second-hand store.

Art for Art's Sake

While fundraising activities and the social aspects of the Alliance were key to the growth and popularity of the organization, many longtime members emphasized the education function of the group. In an interview in early 2008, former president Roberta Walton mentioned the special

Art study group members (from left) Mary Hickam, Mary Mattison, and Lea Cole, with Herron School of Art student Martha Snyder. Photograph from the *Indianapolis Star*, October 18, 1964; courtesy of the *Indianapolis Star*.

kind of women who were attracted to the organization. "They loved the art and other aspects of the Museum," she said.

The Alliance regularly sponsored speakers—many of them internationally known—on design, art collecting, and other topics related to the arts. Among them were Joseph Bloch, Julliard School of Music (March 1963); Henry R. Hope, chairman of the department of fine arts at Indiana University (October 1966); Alfred V. Frankenstein, art and music critic for the *San Francisco Chronicle* (March 1973); Stephen Garrett, architect and first director of the J. Paul Getty Museum (April 1976); artist LeRoy Neiman (March 1977); Perry T. Rathbone, director of Christie's International (March 1978); Olivier Bernier, art historian and lecturer at The Metropolitan Museum of Art (February 1982); interior designer Mark Hampton (October 1982); Rosamond Bernier, lecturer on art and high culture and former *Vogue* editor (September 1985); William J. Williams, education editor and lecturer for the National Gallery of Art (March 1988); chef and author Giuliano Bugialli (February 1994); historian and historic preservationist Roger W. Moss (spring 2002); Fabergé expert Archduke Dr. Géza von Habsburg (spring 2004); and Carleton Varney, interior designer and president of Dorothy Draper & Co. Inc. (March 2007).

Members could also sign up each year for art study groups, which, according to the Alliance yearbook for 1964–65, grew from four in 1961 to thirteen—with 179 members—two years later. In addition to studying a broad range of topics—decoupage, Swedish decoration, and 18th-century flower arrangements are mentioned in one year-end report—the groups also organized occasional "art bus tours" to museums, galleries, and other destinations outside Indianapolis.

The Alliance also offered special series, such as the popular Breakfast in the Courtyard, which featured interior design topics; Art Around Town, which included a lecture, brunch and tour of a collector's home; and the series called "The Art of …," with speakers on subjects ranging from art conservation and appraisals to feng shui.

New Ventures:
The 1980s, 1990s and 2000s

After more than twenty years of successful ventures, the Alliance could have decided to simply maintain the status quo. But they had hundreds of willing volunteers (1,127 as of May 1, 1981), and many of them were newcomers with their own ideas about how they could promote the Museum, bring in new members, and provide financial support.

Among those new ideas was *Indianapolis Collects & Cooks*, which was published by the Alliance in June 1980. It included not only 301 recipes—everything from shrimp dip and Hungarian goulash to pumpkin flan—but also more than forty photographs of art from the Museum's collection. The first printing of 10,000 copies sold out, and a second printing was done in 1985. Linda Charbonneau, the chair of the project, and her committee of volunteers spent more than three years gathering and testing the recipes. Lou (Mrs. Richard O.) Ristine was chairman of the nearly seventy recipe testers and donated her home as a test kitchen for eight months. Charbonneau handled promotion for the cookbook, including appearances on The Bob Braun Show in Cincinnati and on Duffy's Diner with Reid Duffy, reporter and restaurant critic for WRTV, Channel 6.

Programs and special events organized in the early 1980s included Wearable Art `81, a showcase for ten local artists and craftsmen who sold their work through the Alliance Museum Shop. The clothing—modeled by Alliance members—included hand-woven jackets and shawls by Carol Ward; hand-printed, embroidered, and quilted items by Marilyn Price; silk batik clothing by Sue Lyons McFall; and hand-dyed, printed, appliquéd, and quilted clothing by Anne McKenzie Nicholson. Sue Townsend, Alliance president from 1991 to 1993, was a model for the

Georges Lacombe, French, 1868-1916, *Vorhor, The Green Wave*, about 1896-97, egg tempera on canvas, 39 ³/₈ x 28 ³/₈ in., Gift of the Alliance of the Indianapolis Museum of Art, 1984.202

Recipes from *Indianapolis Collects & Cooks*

These recipes are among the 301 included in the Alliance's popular cookbook, first published in 1980 and reprinted in 1985. In his introduction to the book, IMA director Robert A. Yassin wrote: "This book is the culmination of a two and a half year project undertaken with love and with the famous gusto and verve that mark every activity of the Museum's incomparable Alliance."

Fran Harman greets guests at an event promoting the cookbook produced by the Alliance in 1980. IMA Photography Services.

This recipe was submitted by Allen W. Clowes, from his mother's recipe collection.

Lace Cookies

$^1/_2$ cup unsalted butter, melted
$^3/_4$ cup brown sugar, packed, or white sugar
3 tablespoons sifted flour
$^1/_2$ teaspoon salt, scant
1 teaspoon baking powder
1 teaspoon vanilla
1 cup quick oats
1 egg, beaten

Yield: 40 cookies

Mix all ingredients together. Drop $^1/_2$ teaspoonfuls every 3 inches on buttered and *floured* cookie sheet. Bake 7 minutes at 350°F. Wave sheet twelve times before removing cookies with pancake turner. Lovely with Maple Syrup Mousse (page 73 in the cookbook) or ice cream. Freezes well.

The following was submitted by Sylvia Peacock, a longtime member who taught the Lilly House docents.

Chicken in the Old Style

1 fryer, cut up: 3 to 4 lbs.
Salt
Pepper
4 tablespoons olive oil
1 large lime, juice plus grated rind
2 ripe tomatoes, seeded, chopped
3 tablespoons raisins
$^1/_4$ teaspoon oregano
1 onion, chopped
1 garlic clove, chopped
1 medium pineapple or 2 cups crushed canned pineapple
3 teaspoons light rum

Serves 6

Rub lime juice into chicken pieces. Add salt and pepper. Let stand 1 hour. Heat oil; fry chicken until brown. Transfer to casserole with juices. Cover and cook over low heat until barely tender. Add tomatoes, raisins, rind, oregano, onion, and garlic. Cover and cook gently for 10 minutes. Simmer pineapple in saucepan to one-half volume. Add rum and pour over chicken. Serve.

show. "It was a fundraiser and raised awareness of women [working] in textiles arts," Townsend said in an article in the fall 2005 issue of the Museum's magazine, *Previews.* Townsend was co-chair with artist Marge Skreko for a second show a few years later, Art in Motion: Wearable Art '85. The 1985 show eventually traveled to four other venues in Indiana and to the American Association of Museums conference in Detroit that year.

Mary Laux (left), Joanne Lueders, and Linda Charbonneau, chairman of the project, celebrate the publication of the Alliance cookbook *Indianapolis Collects & Cooks.* Photograph from the *Indianapolis Star,* May 23, 1980; courtesy of the *Indianapolis Star.*

By 1983, the Alliance had much to celebrate, not only the Museum's centennial but their own silver anniversary and the completion of their $350,000 pledge for the endowment of the Alliance Sculpture Court. Jo Jameson, who had moved to Georgia, returned to Indianapolis to unveil the commemorative plaque for the space in September that year. In December, *Alliance Acquisitions: Gifts to the IMA,* curated by IMA director Robert Yassin, featured twenty-seven of the more than 200 works of art given by the Alliance over the previous quarter-century. Marion Garmel, art reviewer for the *Indianapolis News,* called the exhibition a "small but fascinating exhibit" and the works on display "choice works indeed," mentioning in particular a Picasso lithograph (*The Goat*), Charles DeMuth's watercolor *Three Pears and a Peach,* and Giovanni Francesco Romanelli's painting *The Finding of Moses,* among others.

In the 1983 annual report, Pam Steele concluded: "Reviewing the last 25 years, the Alliance has grown and changed with the Museum. We have donated over 224 works of art, hundreds of thousands of volunteer hours ... and we have instituted many projects which have stimulated public interest in the Museum and its collections. Excluding the value of the works of art, the

Textile artist Marilyn Price (left) assists Sue Townsend with a jacket featured in the Alliance Wearable Art Show in 1981. IMA Photography Services.

Giovanni Francesco Romanelli, Italian, about 1610-1662, *The Finding of Moses*, about 1657, oil on canvas, 34 x 45 in., Gift of the Alliance of the Indianapolis Museum of Art, 72.18

Alliance has given the Museum over $1,466,500. But always the Museum gives back to the volunteers, the public and our community far more than we can give the Museum."

The group's importance to the Museum as a source of financial support at this point was underscored by Alliance president Dorothy Miller in her report in the 1983-84 yearbook. The Alliance had recently approved a proposal to "restructure" the existing art purchase funds, creating an art endowment fund and two purchase funds. At that point, the Alliance Fine Arts Acquisition Funds, as they came to be called, were the Museum's largest source of money for the purchase of art. The first purchase using the new funds was Jan van Goyen's *The Old Church at Egmond aan Zee*.

Since the Alliance's inception, the art purchase funds have been used to acquire works for every area of the collection, from English silver, furniture, and Dutch paintings to Chinese paintings, African textiles, and contemporary sculpture. By the end of 2007, the Alliance had provided the funds to purchase nearly 300 works of art, either fully or in part. A highlight from recent years is the Alliance's $2.1 million contribution toward the IMA's acquisition of seventy-five masterpieces of Japanese Edo-period painting in 2000. The Alliance also provided funds for the purchase of Moroccan textiles and rugs to round out the IMA's collection in this area for a major exhibition in 2002. Other recent acquisitions made possible by the group's fine arts acquisitions funds include Andy Warhol's screen print *Chicken Noodle* and fashions by Christian Dior and Cristóbal Balenciaga.

Jan van Goyen, Dutch, 1596-1656, *The Old Church at Egmond aan Zee*, 1634, oil on panel, 22 ¼ x 33 ¼ in., Gift of the Alliance of the Indianapolis Museum of Art, 1983.67

By the mid-1980s, the Alliance was humming along like a finely tuned machine. More than 1,000 members were donating thousands of hours in all areas of the Museum, from Lilly Pavilion and the grounds to the information desks and development offices. About half of the volunteers worked in the retail businesses, which were booming. Roberta Walton, in her president's report on 1986–87, noted that the Alliance Museum Shop had realized $80,409 in profit during the year and added that the business had recorded total profits of $887,680 since 1976. The Better Than New Shop, which made $79,155 during the same period, had realized total profits of $907,769 from shop sales and estate sales since its inception in 1973.

Japan, Momoyama period, *Rectangular Dish with Flower*, about 1600, painted buff stoneware with lacquer repairs, 9 9/16 x 8 1/8 in., Gift of the Alliance of the Indianapolis Museum of Art, 1983.1

Andy Warhol, American,
1928-1987, *Chicken Noodle*,
from Campbell's Soup I, 1968,
screen print on smooth white
wove paper, 35 ⅛ x 23 ⅛ in.,
Gift of the Alliance of the
Indianapolis Museum of Art,
2003.79
© 2008 Andy Warhol
Foundation for the Visual
Arts/ARS, New York

Walton also noted another significant change, the addition of three more vice presidents to the Alliance's executive committee, who would provide "much-needed help and support for the many and varied tasks required to effectively run the organization." The four vice presidents were in charge of finance, administration, membership, and projects, and the decision to add these leadership roles was an indication of the scope and importance of the Alliance at this period in its history.

"At that point, we had 1,500 to 2,000 members, we were running all the shops and had other projects," said Walton in the interview in February 2008. "When you have that number of volunteers, you need to be organized. . . . We needed more hands on deck. No one was going to take on the job of the presidency unless they knew they had the help of the vice presidents." And she added, the leadership was looking to the future. "Most of [the Alliance presidents] were brought up through the ranks. . . . They could see how you worked, and then give you more responsibility."

Walton ended her 1986–87 report praising the members: "As the Alliance continues its successful ways, and grows to serve the IMA in new ways, we can all be very proud of this fantastic overall volunteer effort. No job is too big or too small. All are taken on with an enthusiasm unparalleled. As the Museum prepares for growth, so, too, the Alliance is ready to do whatever is necessary to help bring the Museum to the forefront of the Community."

In 1987, for the first time it its history, the Alliance became a major exhibition sponsor with a $100,000 grant for *Art of the Fantastic: Latin America 1920-1987*, and—continuing their tradition as IMA hostesses— the group also organized and funded the gala for the preview of the exhibition. The June event, which drew 1,200 people, included a fashion show by Carolina Herrera, fireworks, the Latin band Som Brasil, and

Tosa Mitsunari, Japanese, 1646-1710, *Birds and Flowers of the Twelve Months*, (pair of six-panel folding screens), Edo period (1600-1868); ink, color, and gold on paper; each 60 ½ in. x 11 ft. 2 ⅞ in., Gift of the Alliance of the Indianapolis Museum of Art, 2000.9 and 2000.10

Oulad Chennane people [?], Oulad Bousbaa people, Arab peoples, Plains of Marrakesh, Morocco, *Rug*, 1925-1950, wool, 142 x 60 ¹/₂ in., Gift of the Alliance of the Indianapolis Museum of Art, 1999.81

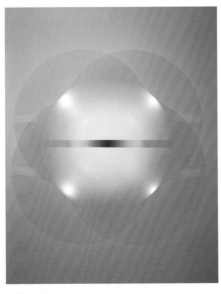

Robert Irwin, American, b. 1928, *Untitled*, 1968-69, lacquer on cast acrylic and tungsten lights, D: 54 in., Gift of the Alliance of the Indianapolis Museum of Art, 1988.220

exotic birds lent by the Indianapolis Zoo. The exhibition and gala were the IMA's contributions to the Pan American Arts Festival, which was held in conjunction with the Tenth Pan American Games, hosted by Indianapolis that summer. "We worked with other sports and arts organizations in the city," said Sue Townsend, who chaired the gala with the assistance of co-chairs Deborah Tolley and Shirley Lewis. "It was a great learning experience."

The IMA looked to the group again in the 1990s for support for exhibitions, including *American Arts & Crafts: Virtue in Design* (1994); *Dutch and Flemish Drawings from the Royal Library, Windsor* and *Italian Paintings from Burghley House* (1995); and *Painting in Spain in the Age of Enlightenment: Goya and His Contemporaries* (1996). They also were a major supporter of the exhibition *Turner Watercolors from Manchester and Indianapolis* (1997) and for the catalogue of the IMA's collection of J.M.W. Turner's watercolors, *Turner in Indianapolis*, published at the same time.

By the end of the 1980s, Alliance leaders were also confident enough in their fundraising abilities to pledge $500,000 to the building fund, for the expansion of the Museum that was to be completed in 1990. (The new Special Events Area was named for the

group to honor the Alliance for the gift.) Mary Sutherland, who led the group as president from 1989 to 1991, noted in her report on her first year in office that the "Project Planning Committee has made a five-year plan of proposed fundraising activities" to fulfill the pledge to the building fund, of which $200,000 had already been paid. It was a formidable task. Membership in the group was down slightly, to 912 members, and the retail businesses had experienced a drop in income, most likely because of construction and renovation of the retail spaces. But she ended on an upbeat note, promising "an aggressive membership push" and predicting that the shops would "rise to new heights as people begin to stream into the new Museum."

Shirley Lewis (left), Deborah Tolley, and Sue Townsend, co-chairmen of the opening night gala committee for *Art of the Fantastic: Latin America, 1920-1987.* Photograph from IMA *Quarterly Magazine,* Summer 1987; IMA Photography Services.

In 1991 the Alliance organized the first International Wine Auction, held in September on the IMA grounds. Individual collectors, wine distributors and wineries donated domestic and European wines for the event, which included both live and silent auctions and a dinner. Other auction items included Baccarat crystal and trips to French and American wine regions. Arie Luyendyk, winner of the 1990 Indianapolis 500, was the honorary chairman for the event, which had a net profit of $40,000.

Sutherland had not been wrong about the Alliance shops, which had record profits in 1992. The Museum Shop alone boasted net income of $158,000. The group also organized multiple events during the same period, including two major fundraisers: Arts and Flowers, "a celebration of floral arts," in late April and the Masterpiece Ball, "A Jewel of an Evening," on December 5. Arts and Flowers, chaired by Helen Dickinson,

Louis Majorelle, French, 1859-1926, *Cabinet*, about 1900; kingwood, mahogany, amaranth, metal hinges, and modern silk; 71 5/8 x 23 1/4 x 18 1/8 in., Purchased in memory of Josephine Cowgill Jameson (Mrs. Booth Tarkington Jameson) by the Alliance of the Indianapolis Museum of Art and Josephine Cowgill Jameson Fund, 1991.42

included indoor and outdoor displays, lectures and an auction. Speakers included Christos Giftos, master floral designer and director of special events at the Metropolitan Museum of Art, and Rosemary Verey, an internationally known author of books on horticulture.

But membership continued to slide and had fallen to 756 by the time Alliance president Judy Rush was writing her report for 1993–94. About half of the members worked in the shops while others pursued new fundraising efforts, with predictable success. In her report, Rush wrote that the second International Wine Auction, held at the Westin Hotel on October 23, 1993, had made $78,700 for the group. "The Chairmen and the committee worked diligently for two years fine tuning the project," she wrote. A wine consultant for the San Francisco auction house Butterfield and Butterfield was auctioneer, and Jean-Michel Cazes—called The Baron of Bordeaux by *Wine Spectator* magazine—was honorary chair.

The Alliance organized four more wine auctions, in 1995, 1997, 1999 and 2002. The 1999 event, co-chaired by Bonita (Bunny) Smith, Jon Jacobson and Jim Arnold, and with comic strip cat Garfield as the honorary chair, produced a net income of $126,206 for the organization. The 2002 auction was held on October 23 at the Westin Hotel, and the black-tie gala included a patrons' reception, silent and live auctions and a dinner. Dennis J. Foley, rare wine consultant for Christie's, San Francisco, was the auctioneer. Rare wines were auctioned along with vacation packages, including a stay at an estate in Tuscany.

In the late 1990s, even as the Alliance membership dwindled, the group's bank accounts only seemed to grow. In her report on 1997, then-president Bunny Smith listed some of the major donations for the year: $75,000 for the J.M.W. Turner exhibition, $30,000 earmarked for the renovation of Oldfields, and the IMA's purchase of Hans Hoffmann's *Radiant Space* using the Alliance's fine arts acquisition funds. The next year, Dorothy Van Hove, in her president's report, listed an $80,000 grant for the exhibition *The Hugenot Legacy* and $70,000 to underwrite a new orientation video for the African galleries. In her report on 2001-02, Gail McDermott-Bowler could boast of art purchases for the African and print collections and a $100,000 donation in support of the exhibition catalogue *Gifts to the Tsars, 1500-1700: Treasures from the Kremlin.*

McDermott-Bowler also had good news to record in the 2002-03 annual report. "It was with a great deal of pride that the Alliance allocated funds in excess of $300,000 to underwrite a series of publications celebrating the New IMA." The first book, *Oldfields*, which records the history of the estate and the two families that had once lived there, was published in October 2004. The second, *Indianapolis Museum of Art: Highlights of the Collection*, came out in the spring of 2005, just in time for the grand opening of the renovated and expanded museum. The third, an extensive history of the Museum—*Every Way Possible: 125 Years of the Indianapolis Museum of Art*—was published in fall 2008 as part of the celebration of the IMA's founding in 1883.

Vito Acconci, American, b. 1940, *Round Trip (A Space to Fall Back On)*, 1975; stools, boxes, and audio tape; 15 x 12 x 8 ft. installed, Gift of the Alliance of the Indianapolis Museum of Art, 1989.35

Yoruba people, Republic of Benin, Western Africa, *Egungun Masquerade Costume*, mid-1900s; velvet, leather, cotton, wool, sequins, beads, metallic threads, and cowrie shells, L: 68 in.; Gift of the Alliance of the Indianapolis Museum of Art, 1992.67

Among other highlights of 2002–03, McDermott-Bowler included the Alliance's commissioning of a 14-carat gold-filled charm, a project conceived and managed by former president Elizabeth Coffey. The charm, which was also a pin, was based on the design of the Sutphin Fountain, a familiar IMA logo that had been a part of the Alliance's own logo for many years. Income from sales of the charm, which was proudly sported by Alliance members, was used to benefit the Museum.

"Challenges and changes" were the focus of Patricia Ritz's report on her first year as president, 2003–04. "The Alliance has been faced with the challenges of finding innovative and exciting fundraising projects and expanding and retaining our membership. Committees to address both these concerns have been created and will be working toward creative solutions. We view these challenges as our opportunities to revisit the

Pakistan, Gandharan period, 1st-5th century, head of Buddha, 3rd-4th century, stucco with paint, 15 ³/₄ x 7 ³/₄ x 7 ¹/₄ in., Gift of the Alliance of the Indianapolis Museum of Art, 1994.1

Edo people, Benin kingdom, Nigeria, Western Africa, *Container Lid in the Form of a Leopard Face*, 1500-1600, brass, H: 7 ³/₄ in., Gift of the Alliance of the Indianapolis Museum of Art, 1992.61

Robert Scott Duncanson, American, 1821-1872, *Loch Long*, 1867, oil on canvas, 20 ¹/₂ x 33 ³/₄ in., Gift of the Alliance of the Indianapolis Museum of Art, 1997.142

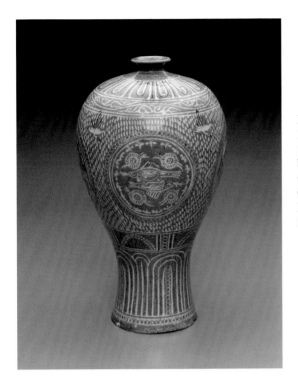

Korea, Choson period,
1392-1911, *Maebyong*, about
1400, stoneware with inlaid
black and white slip under
transparent glaze, H: 12 ½ in.,
Gift of the Alliance of the
Indianapolis Museum of Art,
2001.223

William Callow,
English, 1812-1908,
*Glacier du Rhone and the
Galenstock from the
Furka Pass Road*, 1848,
watercolor over pencil
on off-white wove
paper, 22 x 30 in.
(image and sheet),
Gift of the Alliance of
the Indianapolis
Museum of Art,
2005.3

mission of the Alliance, assess our capabilities, and renew our commitment to the IMA in new, meaningful and positive ways." It was the group's forty-fifth year.

Over the next three years, Alliance members faced rapid and dramatic changes that proved to be daunting. The seventh biennial wine auction, scheduled for October 9, 2004, was canceled in the spring of that year because of concerns that it would conflict with the Museum's Founders' Day celebration on October 11. In January 2006, the Museum took over the management of the Alliance's popular and very successful Museum Shop (now The IMA Store). One project that endured was the Better Than New Shop, which continued to draw loyal patrons and to raise

Alliance members model Lilly Pulitzer fashions from the Pink Lime store at the spring luncheon on March 20, 2006. From left, Sharon Paskins, Davine Nolcox, Wilma Borinstein, Dorothy Miller, Jackie Jacobs, and Gail McDermott-Bowler. Photograph from Alliance President's book, 2005–2007, Alliance archives.

Charles Frederick Worth, English, 1825-1895, *Imperial Russian Court Dress*, about 1888; silk lamé moiré, silk velvet, embroidered with clear glass crystals, silver sequins, silver foil, silver strips; skirt: L: 47 ½ in.; bodice: L: 14 in.; train: 130 x 60 in.; Gift of the Alliance of the Indianapolis Museum of Art, 2006.3a-c

Alliance presidents at the Celebration Tea in June 2005. From left, back row: Dorothy Van Hove, Shirley Kulwin (president that year), Elizabeth Coffey, Patricia Ritz, and Gail McDermott-Bowler. Seated, from left: Dorothy Miller and Fran Harman. © Randy Johnson Photography.

substantial sums ($100,200 in 2003), most of which was used to replenish the fine arts acquisition funds. But by the end of 2007, and at the request of the Museum, the shop had closed. It was the last of the group's long-term fundraising projects, and the end of an era for the group. In the meantime, all IMA affiliates were being encouraged to focus on volunteering and their education functions and to curtail their efforts as fundraisers.

With their mission changing, Alliance members found purpose in Alliance traditions. Learning about art in all its variety was, in particular, still an important part of Alliance membership. In her president's report for 2005–06, Shirley Kulwin described the highlights of the year: the Holiday Tea in Deer Zink Pavilion, visits to the studios of local artists, a day trip to Wakefield Scearce Galleries, in Kentucky—known for their English antiques—and, for the spring program, a lecture on couture and a fashion show featuring Lilly Pulitzer designs. And while fundraising was no longer part of their mission, the group welcomed opportunities to provide financial support to the IMA. Kulwin reported on the group's latest gift of art, a gown designed by the legendary French designer Charles Frederick Worth for the granddaughter of Tsar Nicholas I of Russia. It was a fitting gift from a group that had been known for its elegant balls.

From left: Alliance president Ginger Hoyt; Fran Harman; Maxwell Anderson, the Melvin & Bren Simon Director and CEO of the IMA, and Pam Hicks, at the fiftieth anniversary celebration in April 2008. Photograph by Geordana Davis.

Ginger Hoyt, in her president's message for the Alliance's fiftieth year set the tone for the days ahead: "This year and next [2007 and 2008] will require us to keep up with the many changes and transitions the Museum will be requiring of all of its affiliate organizations. We expect to accomplish all challenges with enthusiasm and grace."

Enthusiasm and grace were among the qualities that distinguished the Alliance during their first fifty years, when so much was asked of them. In an interview in early 2008, former Alliance president Patricia Ritz paid tribute to all the members who had preceded her: "They were the hostesses, the social chairmen, the fundraisers all those years. . . . Their events were incredible." And she added, "They took it very, very seriously."

Ritz also noted that, in addition to their contributions as part of the Alliance, many of the members made their own individual contributions over the years, including generous financial support and gifts of art. Others served the Museum in multiple volunteer roles. Among them were Laura Jolly, who served as secretary of the IMA board of governors for seven years, and Anna White, who served as board secretary from 1986 to 1990 and as IMA chairman from 1990 to 1993. Following her tenure as president, Marian Meditch was appointed by Mayor Richard Lugar to

Ginger Hoyt, 2007–08 Alliance president, and Pam Hicks, vice president of administration and president-elect, with thirteen past presidents at the fiftieth anniversary celebration in April 2008. Front row, from left: Mary Sutherland, Jeanne Scofield, Fran Harman, Patricia Ritz (behind Harman), Anna White, Dorothy Van Hove, Dorothy Miller, Laura Jolly, Shirley Kulwin, Pam Steele, Roberta Walton, IMA deputy director of public affairs Leann Standish, and IMA manager of affiliate and volunteer services Amber Laibe. Back row, left to right: Hicks, Linda Charbonneau, Hoyt, and Gail McDermott-Bowler. Photograph by Geordana Davis.

serve as a representative of the City of Indianapolis on the Museum's executive board. Meditch also served an eight-year term as a member of the Indiana Arts Commission. For many years, until 2006, the Alliance president served as a representative trustee on the Museum's board.

In the 2005 *Previews* article that featured past Alliance presidents, several mentioned the friendships they had formed as a crucial aspect of their Alliance experience. "What was most important was the friends I made," said Jolly. McDermott-Bowler mentioned making new friends "among some very intelligent and capable women."

"There is a closeness, a bond among these women that has been a big part of it," said Ritz. And as 2008 came to a close, that bond—and the Alliance—endured. A survey had been sent to members earlier in the year, and of those who responded, the majority felt that it was important for the Alliance to continue, with an emphasis on educational and social programs, and to redefine its mission for the next half-century.

Founder and First Lady

Mrs. Booth Tarkington Jameson. It was just the kind of name that could open doors in Indianapolis during the 1950s. And Josephine Cowgill Jameson, or just "Jo," as she was known to her friends, made good use of it in her efforts to attract new members and support for the John Herron Art Museum. Her husband was the nephew of the popular American novelist Booth Tarkington, and Jameson credits "Uncle Booth" with introducing her to the Museum. Tarkington was a long-time member himself, and later a trustee and chairman of the Museum's Fine Arts Committee, and Jameson said that he gave her a membership in the Art Association of Indianapolis soon after she was married, in the early 1930s.

But her vital role in the Museum's history would not be defined until years later. After the death of her husband in 1956, she took some advice from a friend that would set her on a career path. In an article by Mary Waldon Butler in the September 2, 1973, issue of the *Indianapolis Star*, Jameson recounted the story: She was having lunch with Mrs. Arthur W. (Nell) Herrington, who asked her, "What are you going to do with your life? . . . What are you interested in?" "Art and the museum" was Jameson's reply. Encouraged by Herrington to "make a job" for herself at the Museum, Jameson put together a plan for luring new members and volunteers and convinced Wilbur Peat, the Museum's director at the time, that the Art Association needed a public relations secretary. A year later, and with the help of Virginia Ansted and Beverly Carmichael, she would launch the Herron Museum Alliance.

Jameson's credentials included more than just the Tarkington connection and her many years of membership in the Art Association. In the *Star* article she talked about her education and early interest in art. The daughter of a wealthy Terre Haute manufacturer, she attended school

Walter Stein, American, b. 1924, *Portrait of Josephine Cowgill Jameson*, 1973, oil on canvas, 80 ½ x 68 ½ in.; Gift of the Alliance of the Indianapolis Museum of Art, 73.176

in Germany when she was eight years old and made some of her first visits to art museums there. She later attended the Elmhurst boarding school in Connersville, Indiana, where she took a course in art history taught by the school's headmistress "that made a terrific impression on me. Years later, when I went to Europe, I had to choose between going to the races and seeing the Queen of England or going to the National Museum and seeing the Elgin Marbles the headmistress had told me about. I chose the marbles." She attended Indiana University and Swarthmore College and graduated from Cornell University with a degree in English and history. She even studied piano at the Julliard School in New York City. She taught English for a short time at Emmerich Manual Training High School in Indianapolis before she married Booth Jameson.

She was also active in the Junior League of Indianapolis and was president from 1939 to 1940. She was president of the Indianapolis Woman's Club from 1958 to 1959, and of the Progressive Club from 1959 to 1960. At the Museum, she was a member of the School Committee of the Art Association when Caroline Marmon Fesler was the chairman.

In an article written by Jane Moore Howe for the *Indianapolis Star Magazine*, November 10, 1963, Jameson described the duties of her art museum position, which she sometimes referred to as "membership secretary": "It is more than a 9 to 5 job. I try to see prospective members in a casual way. I bring guests and serve as unofficial hostess at all Museum members' affairs." Among the activities she organized for members were bus trips to museums in St. Louis, Cleveland, Chicago, and Cincinnati and a "coffee chat" series that was popular for many years. She was also instrumental in the founding of the Decorative Arts Society, Horticultural Society and the Asian Art Society at the Museum.

Fran Harman, who had been a member of the Alliance for almost fifty years, knew Jameson well. "She had a persuasive personality," she said in a 2008 interview. It was a trait that made Jameson an ideal candidate for her job. She was also known for her stylish hats and high society airs, which artist Walter Stein successfully captured in the portrait he made of her in 1973. In Mary Waldon Butler's 1973 article, Harman explained: "Jo Jameson is regal, but not austere—not Jo. She is so warm and friendly. New members always are endeared to her, for she seems to take each under her wing."

Linda Charbonneau, who worked as a volunteer for Jameson in the membership office, recalled her strategic use of her well-known name. "She was a grande dame, in the truest sense of the word," said Charbonneau. "But she was very nice too."

Jameson moved to Thomasville, Georgia, in 1981, but her friends in the Alliance never forgot her. She returned in 1983 to unveil the dedicatory plaque for the Alliance Sculpture Court and to celebrate the Alliance's twenty-fifth year. She died January 19, 1991. And she no doubt would have been pleased with the headline on the obituary that appeared in the *Indianapolis Star*: "Booth Tarkington kin Josephine F. Jameson founded art alliance."

Alliance Presidents
1958-2009

Lucille Martindale,* 1958-1959

Virginia Ansted,* 1959-1960

Betty Buschmann,* 1960-1961

Esther Gerdan,* 1961-1962

Irving Springer,* 1962-1963

Kay DeBoest,* 1963-1964

Beverly Carmichael, 1964-1965
  [Beverly (Mrs. Ellis) Bradley]

Jean Miner,* 1965-1966

Margie Tomlinson,* 1966-1967

Marian Meditch, 1967-1969

Jane Dutton,* 1969-1971

Fran Harman, 1971-1973

Linda Charbonneau, 1973-1975

Jeanne Scofield, 1975-1977

Anna White, 1977-1979

Elizabeth Lawton,* 1979-1981

Dorothy Miller, 1981-1983

Pam Steele, 1983-1985

Roberta Walton, 1985-1987

Laura Jolly, 1987-1989

Mary Sutherland, 1989-1991

Sue Townsend, 1991-1993

Judy Rush, 1993-1995

Elizabeth Coffey, 1995-1997

Bonita (Bunny) Smith,* 1997-1999

Dorothy Van Hove, 1999-2001

Martha Stiers,* president-elect 2001

Gail McDermott-Bowler, 2001-2003

Patricia Ritz, 2003-2005

Shirley Kulwin, 2005-2007

Ginger Hoyt, 2007-2009

*deceased

Index